NURTURING EMOTIONAL INTELLIGENCE IN CHILDREN

IN CHILDREN

A PRACTICAL GUIDE FOR PARENTS

WRITTEN BY
BHAVANA NAGENDRA

ILLUSTRATED BY
SURA SHARMA

ISBN 979-8-89186-449-8

FOREWORD

—By *Dr. Noor Fathima, Psychologist, Behavioural Scientist, Coach and Thought Leader at BrainWav Consulting*

In our fast-paced, ever-changing world, one thing remains constant: the profound impact of emotional intelligence on our children's lives. As parents, we all desire to see our children grow into confident, resilient, and empathetic individuals who can gracefully understand life's challenges. This desire makes the parenting journey both incredibly rewarding and, at times, utterly bewildering.

"Nurturing Emotional Intelligence in Children" is not just another parenting book. It's a heartfelt exploration into the world of emotions and how we, as parents, can empower our children to master them. Drawing on the latest research in psychology, and child development, this book delves into the profound significance of emotional intelligence and its undeniable connection to success, happiness, and healthy relationships.

This book by Bhavana Nagendra is a practical guide to building a foundation of trust, connection, and understanding that will serve as a lifelong gift to your child. As parents, we know that every moment counts. "Nurturing Emotional Intelligence in Children" will help you make those moments count in the most meaningful way possible, guiding you through the beautiful journey of raising emotionally intelligent children who are prepared to embrace life's challenges with confidence and compassion.

As a psychologist with over two decades of work and experience in dealing with parents and children, I strongly feel that this book is indeed the need of the hour. It will help parents embark on a transformative journey that will not only shape their child's future but also deepen the bond between you and your little one. "Nurturing Emotional Intelligence in Children" is here to remind you that the most profound life lessons often learned within the walls of our own homes are lessons of the heart.

Praise for the Book

An absolute gem for parents! 'Nurturing Emotional Intelligence in Children' is a must-read guide offering profound insights and practical advice on raising emotionally intelligent children. It is an exceptional resource for parents as it provides a roadmap for building emotional solid foundations in our kids, enabling them to thrive in an increasingly complex world.

As a psychologist, I wholeheartedly recommend it to all parents seeking to raise compassionate, self-aware and resilient children. The author's understanding and practical approach offer a refreshing perspective on parenting that emphasises connection, communication, and empathy. This book is a true gift to parents everywhere.

INTRODUCTION

Identifying, understanding, and managing emotions is the key to personal, professional and spiritual development.

This book aims to equip you to nurture emotional intelligence in yourself to deal with the people around you. More than all the other roles I have to take on, daily being a Parent feels closest to my heart. From where I stand, being a parent means being responsible for the little humans to be emotionally healthy, well-connected with themselves, resilient, and self-reliant.

While all of us are born with and are capable of being human, the above attributes, life experiences, social conditioning, cultural influences, and lifestyle choices distance us from nurturing our emotional intelligence.

All of the suggestions in the book, be it getting help for overcoming the impact of challenging life experiences, lifestyle changes, unlearning the conditioned fear response, setting & respecting boundaries, creating a safe space, unstructured time for reflection, expression without hesitation, and even listening are ones I have implemented on myself to be able to create an environment that nurtures emotional intelligence in my child.

While there is a long way to go, as a parent and a person, I have seen value in nurturing my emotional health and deepening my connection with myself because:

- This is a choice model for my daughter, who now knows that focusing on nurturing herself emotionally is important

- It helps me be emotionally available and present in all my roles and relationships, be it as a parent, a partner, a friend, a colleague, and a coach

- It allows me to focus on my goals personally and professionally without a clouded sense of judgement and ask for help if I need it

- It has given me the confidence to set boundaries and ensure I firmly communicate my discomfort with people who trespass

- It has shifted my thoughts from self-doubt, anger, and anxiety to self-acceptance, kindness towards myself and gratitude

THIS BOOK IS FOR:

- Anyone who is looking to work on nurturing their emotional health and deepening their connection with themselves for personal and professional growth

- Parents who want to create an environment to develop emotional health and resilience in children

- Teachers, facilitators and anyone else who works with children and would like to focus on the child's holistic development

- Anyone who is looking to develop a strong relationship with their spouse/ partner to create a healthy family environment

WELCOME

to the wonderful world of parenthood! It is one of the most life-changing and rewarding experiences you will have. We are so glad you have chosen us to help guide you through this very special time. This manual is intended to give your family some extra guidance and general information in order to help you enjoy this journey with your child.

One of the major challenges of being a parent is going through a journey unconditioning and unlearning to connect with yourself. At Svadhyaya we do just that!

Svadhyaya means 'Journey to Self'. Svadhyaya is a space specifically created for parents, young adults and everyone else who would like to go through a journey of unconditioning and unlearning to connect with yourself.

Wondering how this helps?

In today's world a lot is being said about doing what you love to be happy and successful. While this is true, the hardest part for most people is to identify what they love, and the biggest problem is that the sole measure for happiness and success being the material in nature. Every ancient philosophy talks about how each of us is born with a purpose. It is in finding this purpose and true joy (and in today's context material success) is felt in working towards fulfilling that purpose.

At Svadhyaya we believe that one must go through a journey of self-reflection of their experiences, patterns, values, beliefs, and lifestyle to understand themselves better – a 'Journey to Self' to begin a journey of where one's body, mind, heart, and spirit are in harmony. It is from this state of consciousness that we start working towards identifying your purpose (goal) that is aligned with your passion, skills, and needs!
As a Parent, being in this state of harmony and consciousness is the best gift one can give their child.

TABLE OF
CONTENT

WHAT IS
EMOTIONAL
INTELLIGENCE?

WHAT DOES
LACK OF EMOTIONAL
INTELLIGENCE
LOOK LIKE?

WHAT ARE THE
FACTORS THAT INHIBIT
DEVELOPMENT
OF SOCIAL
INTELLIGENCE
IN CHILDREN?

HOW TO DEVELOP
EMOTIONAL
INTELLIGENCE
IN CHILDREN?

WHAT IS THE
IMPACT OF
EMOTIONAL
INTELLIGENCE?

WHAT ARE THE
LEVELS OF
EMOTIONAL
INTELLIGENCE?

WHAT
LIFESTYLE
CHOICE
HELP BUILD
EMOTIONAL
INTELLIGENCE?

HOW DO WE FRAME A
RESPONSE
WHILE DEALING
WITH A CHILD'S
EMOTIONS?

WHAT IS
EMOTIONAL INTELLIGENCE?

Emotional intelligence is the ability to perceive, reason, understand, manage, and use emotions to communicate with and relate to others effectively and constructively.

What Are The Components Of Emotional Intelligence?
Emotional intelligence is commonly defined by four attributes:

SELF AWARENESS

The ability to recognise one's emotions and how they affect our thoughts and behaviour. The ability to identify one's strengths and weaknesses.

SELF REGULATED

The ability to respond rather than react, healthy management of emotions, taking the initiative, honouring commitments, and adapting to changes.

SELF DIRECTED

The ability to identify one's goals, create a plan of action and implement it to achieve them. They also know when to stop and ask for help.

EMPATHY

The ability to perceive other people's emotions, needs, concerns, emotional cues, and being socially comfortable.

RELATIONSHIP MANAGEMENT

The ability to build & maintain good relationships, communicate effectively, inspire positively, collaborate, and manage conflict through healthy communication channels and boundaries.

EMOTIONAL INTELLIGENCE OR THE LACK THERE OF

LOOK LIKE?

Let's look at the attributes in more detail below with examples based on psychologist and writer Daniel Goleman's five key components.

SELF AWARENESS

Self-awareness refers to one's awareness of thoughts and feelings, and Self-awareness refers to one's ability to be aware of their thoughts, feelings, and behaviours. Self-aware people understand why they think, feel, and act as they do. People with low self-awareness need help in understanding their feelings and reactions. The right kind of help can develop awareness among these people.

A Manager is trying to explain something to the team. The team needed help following the explanation as the Manager veered off the subject.

High EI:
The person realises they can sometimes go off on a tangent, so they apologise and start again.

Low EI:
The person becomes frustrated when their co-worker is not following their words because they are not paying attention.

SELF REGULATION

Self-regulation is the ability to control and manage emotions appropriately. This is possible only when a person is aware bout their feelings. Self-regulation allows a person to respond in a healthy & helpful manner rather than impulsively react to circumstances. People with low self-regulation tend to have emotional outbursts and impulsive reactions.

A customer orders food at a restaurant. The food takes longer than usual to arrive, and when it does, it is the wrong dish.

High EI: The person is slightly disappointed but understands that the restaurant is busy and has a high chance of errors. They calmly speak to the person serving and work towards fixing the order.

Low EI: The individual is frustrated and can think of nothing but blame the person serving for the issue.

SELF DIRECTED

Being self-directed is a person's intent to achieve specific goals. They work towards succeeding and improving themselves. They value personal development over immediate reward. Low emotional intelligence can surface as constantly missing deadlines for accomplishing goals and not taking responsibility for them.

A person hopes to open a cafe one day.

High EI: Sets realistic and achievable goals and takes baby steps to open the restaurant.

Low EI: Sets their sight on the goal but cannot accomplish the tasks required to open the restaurant within planned timelines.

EMPATHY

Empathy is the ability to understand another individual's feelings or situation from the individual's point of view. Self-awareness plays a vital role in developing empathy.

A person with low levels of empathy does not understand how others feel and how their actions might affect others.

A person's friend is under pressure about an upcoming test and chooses not to join the person for a movie.

High EI: The person listens to their friend's concerns and offers to help in any manner the friend needs.

Low EI: The person takes it personally and gets upset about the friend not joining them for a movie.

SOCIAL SKILLS

Social skills are the ability to have helpful interactions with others and build healthy relationships. A person with poor social skills may need help communicating with others and building or maintaining primary relationships.

A friend introduces a person to their partner.

High EI: The person makes their friend's partner feel welcome and included.

Low EI: The person makes a friend's partner feel like an outsider and does not notice their friend's discomfort with the predicament.

Over the next few days, list five situations that emotionally challenge you and identify which attributes were active and which switched off.

SITUATION	SELF AWARENESS	SELF REGULATED	SELF DIRECTED	EMPATHY	RELATIONSHIP MANAGEMENT

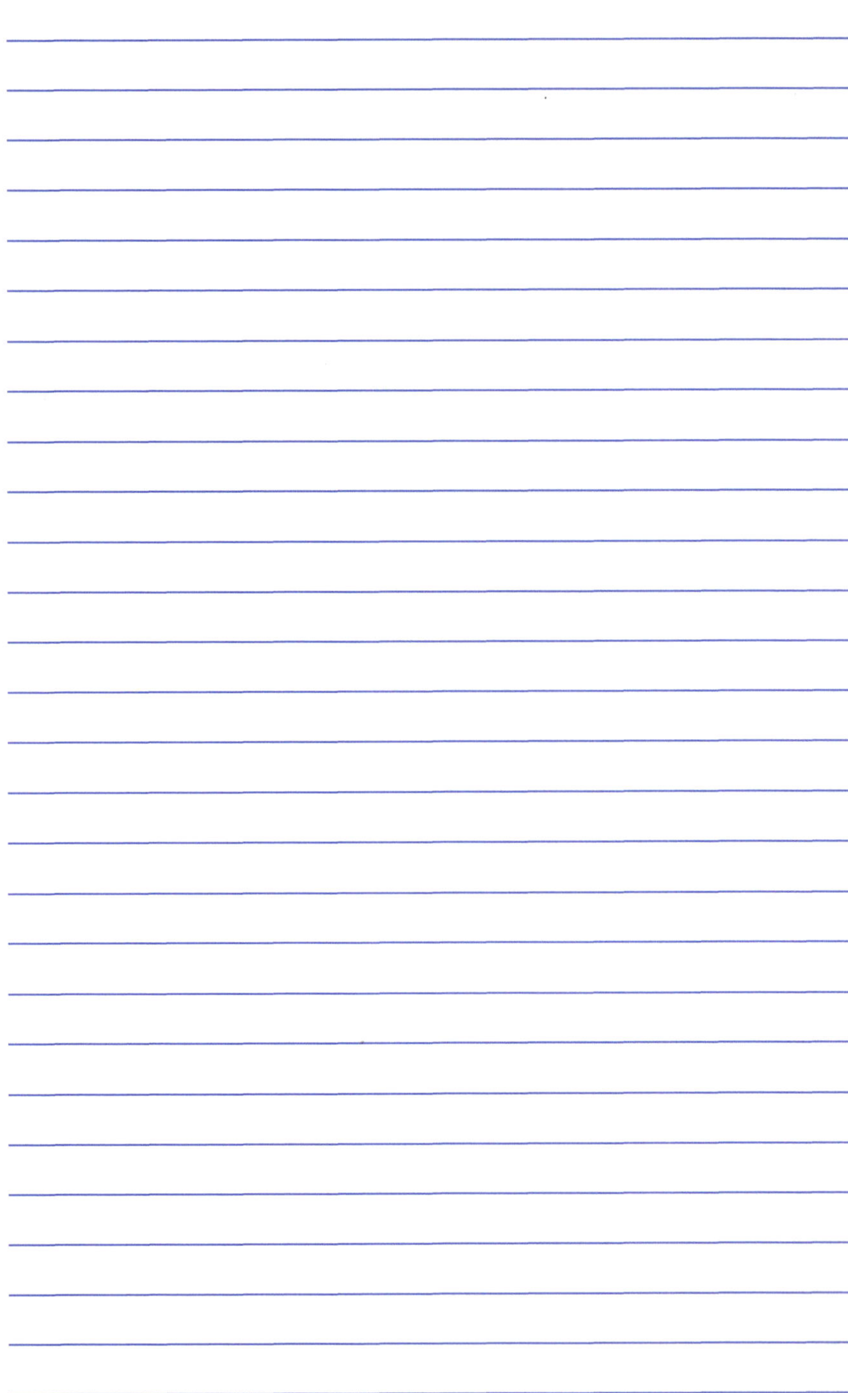

IMPACT OF EMOTIONAL INTELLIGENCE

THINKING BEFORE REACTING

Emotionally intelligent people know emotions can be powerful and would take time before responding. This ripple effect allows everyone else to regulate their emotions, reason and respond.

GREATER SELF AWARENESS

Emotionally intelligent people understand and manage their emotions appropriately.

EMPATHY FOR OTHERS

·Emotionally intelligent individuals consider other people's perspectives, experiences, and emotions and use this information to explain why people behave the way they do.

For each of the five situations, elaborate on your response. Remember, at this stage, there is no right or wrong.

The exercise is to help you understand yourself better based on your thoughts, feelings and actions in varied situations.

Situation	Identify if it was a response or a reaction	Identify how you feel about it now

NOTES

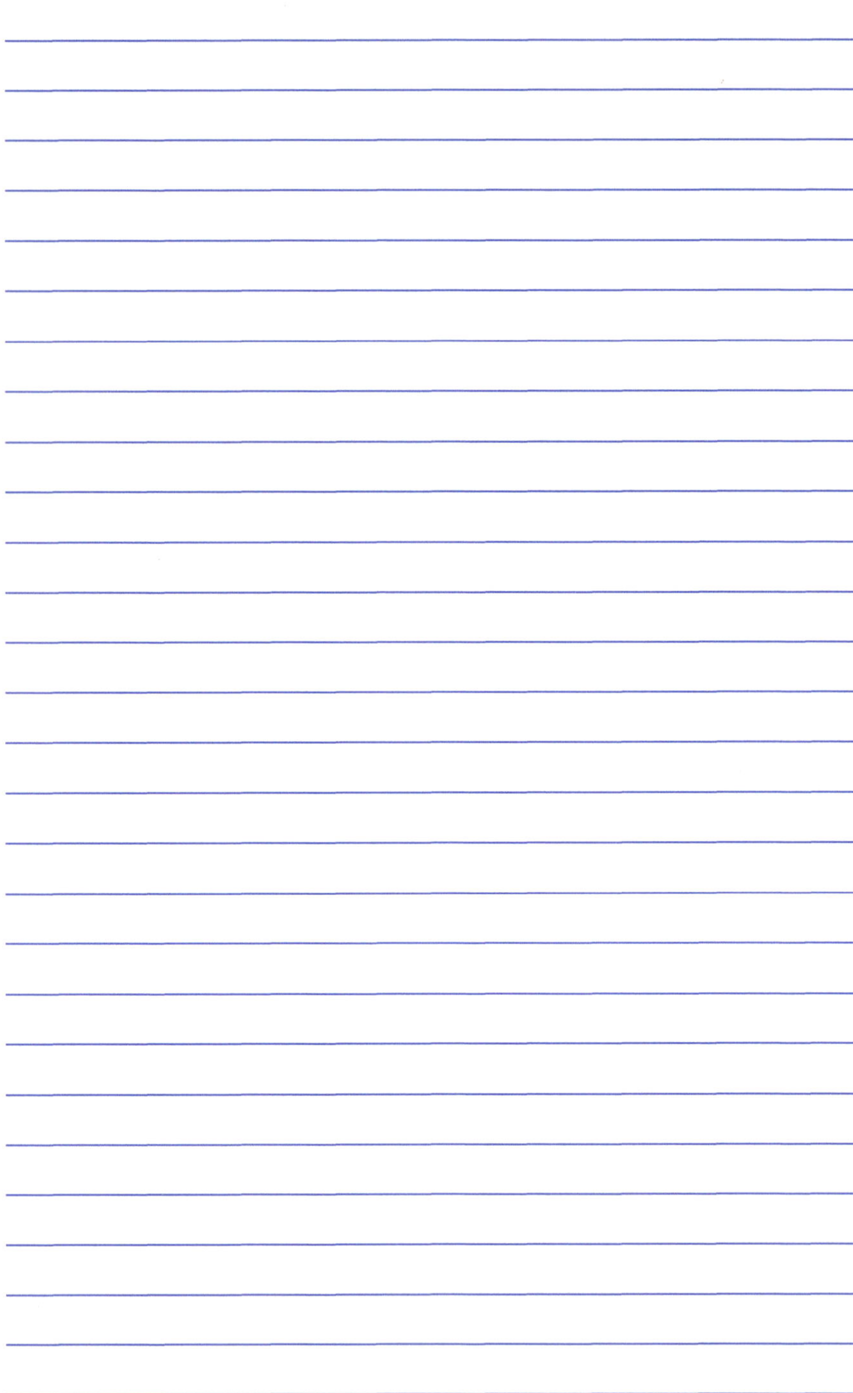

DEVELOPMENT OF SOCIAL INTELLIGENCE

IN CHILDREN

Some significant causes of anxiety include events or circumstances that lead to changes in the brain chemistry, i.e., excessive production of stress hormones like cortisol.

LIFE SITUATIONS

A child's exposure to stressful and challenging events such as losing a loved one, serious illness, bullying, violence, or abuse.

LEARNED BEHAVIOURS:

A child's exposure to a fear- or anxiety-inducing environment can "teach" them to be anxious.

LIFESTYLE CHOICE

A child's exposure to inappropriate food choices, too much screen time, lack of playtime outdoors, or connection with nature.

 **How many of them can you change or eliminate from the environment?**

 **How do they impact you, to what extent?**

 **How do they impact your children, to what extent?**

 **How many of them can you change or eliminate from the environment? What resources would you require for it?**

What support would you need for you and your children for the factors you can't change or control?

NOTES

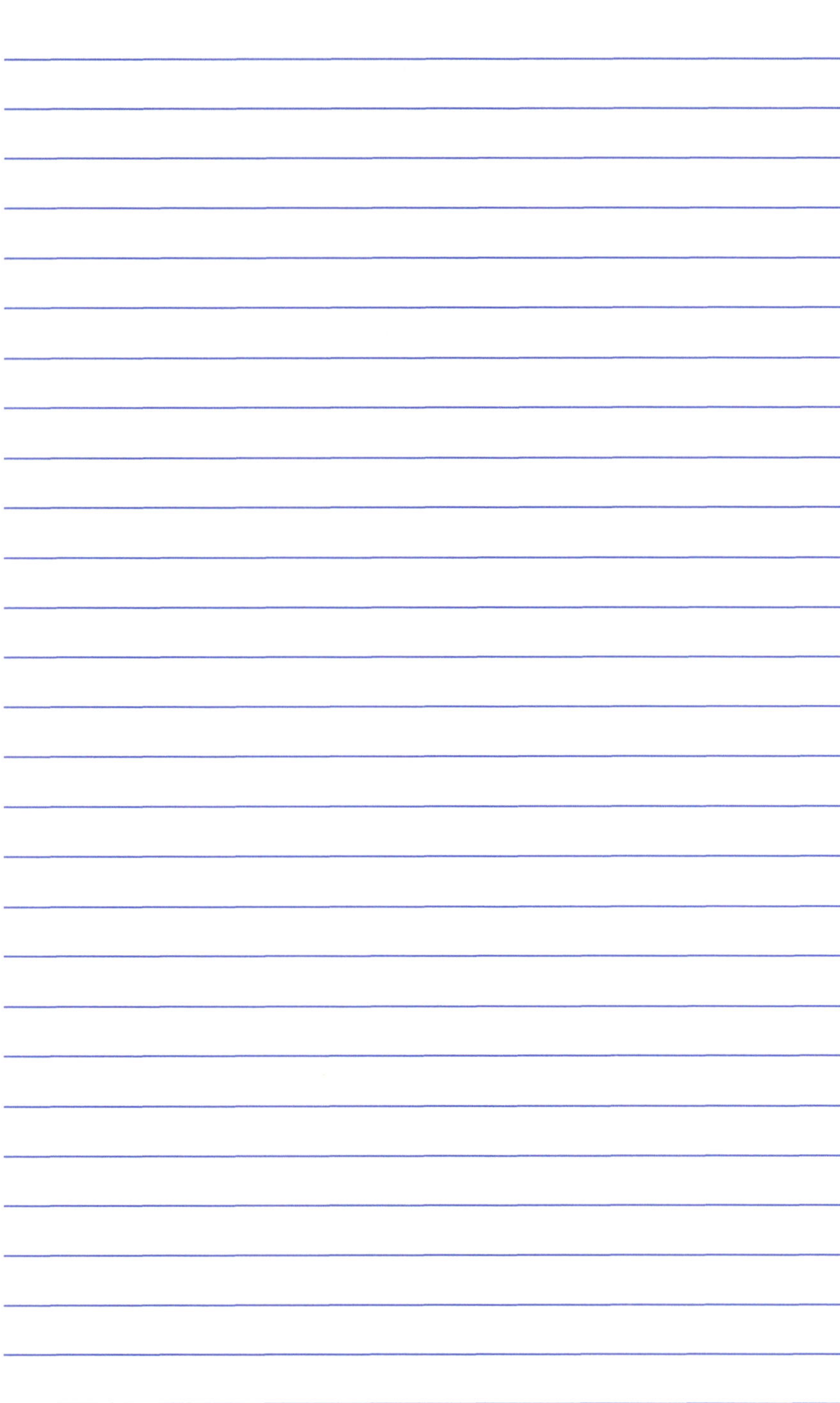

LEVELS OF EMOTIONAL INTELLIGENCE

1. PERCEIVING EMOTIONS

Perceiving emotions accurately through nonverbal signals, including body language, facial expressions, tone of speech and the like.

2. REASONING WITH EMOTIONS

This involves using emotions to manage thoughts and cognitive activity, i.e. responding over reacting.

3. UNDERSTANDING EMOTIONS

Understanding emotions is interpreting the cause of the emotions.

4. MANAGING EMOTIONS

Managing emotions is the highest level of emotional intelligence. At this level of emotional intelligence, one can regulate their emotions and respond appropriately to others' emotions.

Use the feeling wheel on the next page list out all the emotions you felt during the 5 situations, and for each emotion, identify the levels you were able to reach.

SITUATION	EMOTIONS	1	2	3	4

FEELING

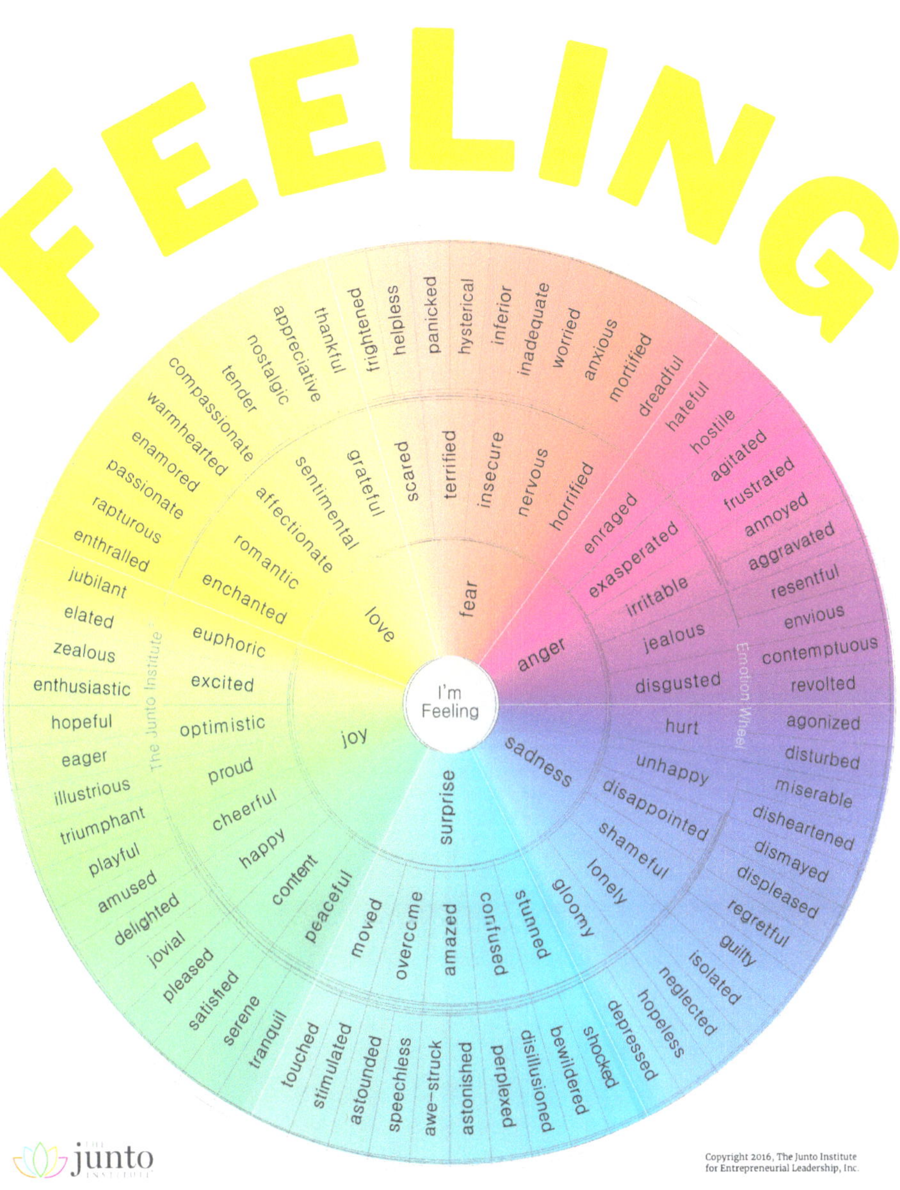

WHEEL

NOTES

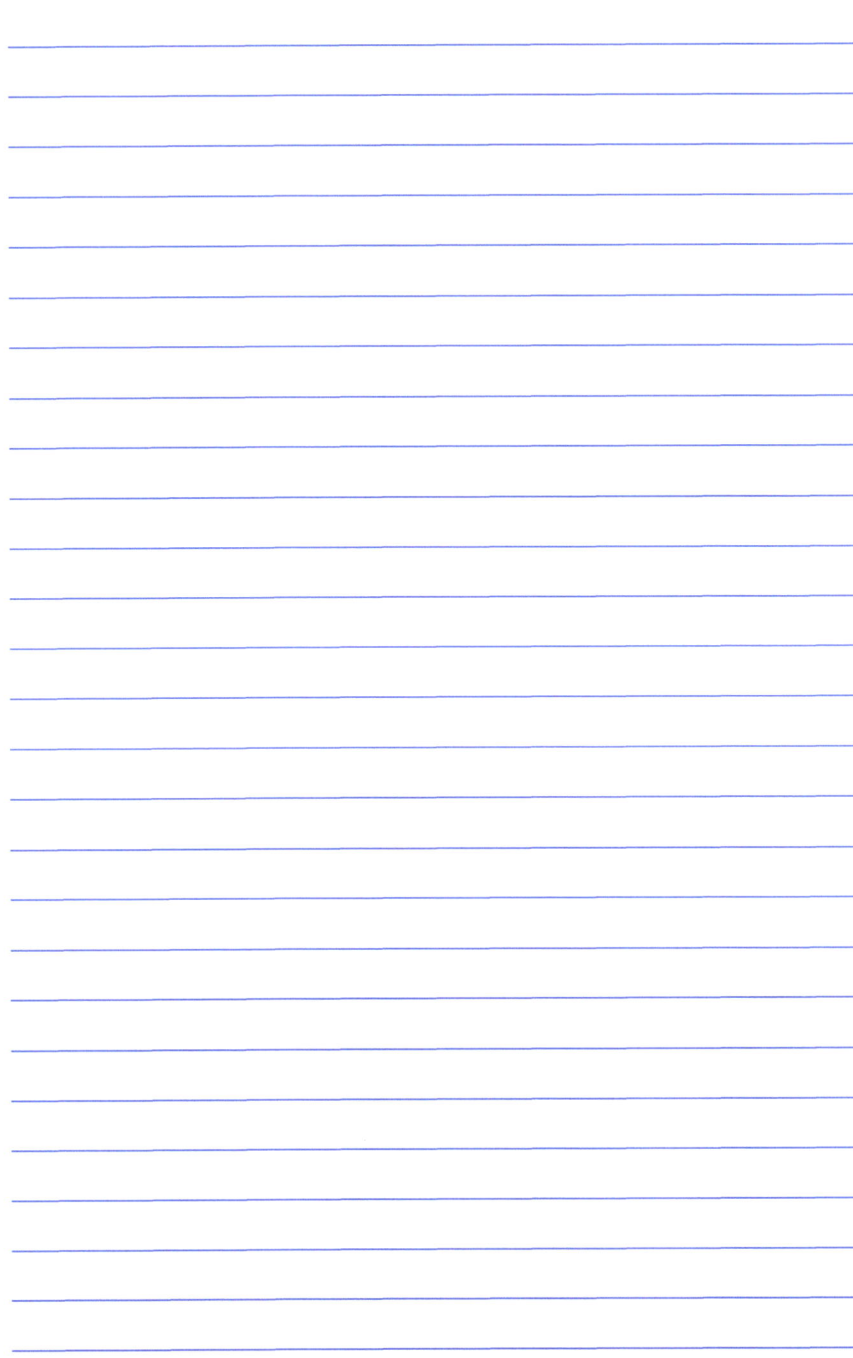

WHAT **LIFESTYLE CHOICES**
HELP BUILD EMOTIONAL INTELLIGENCE IN CHILDREN

As parents, our primary focus should be creating a healthy and conducive environment for a child to express, manage and overcome stressful situations. We can incorporate a few things into a child's life to ensure healthy stress management

MOVEMENT

Depending on age, Children need between one hour to three hours of physical activity. Physical activity can be structured activities like exercise routines like yoga, a sport, a martial art form, a dance form, or unstructured play time involving movement. Either way, the time spent should focus more on the movement and less on performance or goal-oriented learning.

RISK PLAY

What seemed to have been the natural course of play for millennials and the generations before them, such as climbing high objects, swinging high into the air, using actual tools, hide and seek, and the like, is now classified under risky play. These are the kind of games that can put the child at physical risk. Creating opportunities for children to indulge in risky play allows them to strategise, face challenges, promote risk management skills, develop self-confidence, and increase resilience. More importantly, it makes them more aware of their body and mind! Risky play can be made a part of their movement time.

CONNECTION WITH NATURE

Connection with nature can happen outdoors or with natural materials such as soil, natural colours & clay. Being in touch with natural elements promotes a healthy stress-resilient immune system and mental health. So, schedule time for play in an outdoor park or a simple hike, create a small garden patch, incorporate natural art materials, or engage them in cooking and cleaning dishes! Outdoor time can be combined with movement & risky play.

MUSIC

Music has always been known for its ability to soothe, relax, uplift our mood, and improve concentration, even through just listening. Music can be incorporated through structured music lessons, simply playing soothing music at home, or combining both.

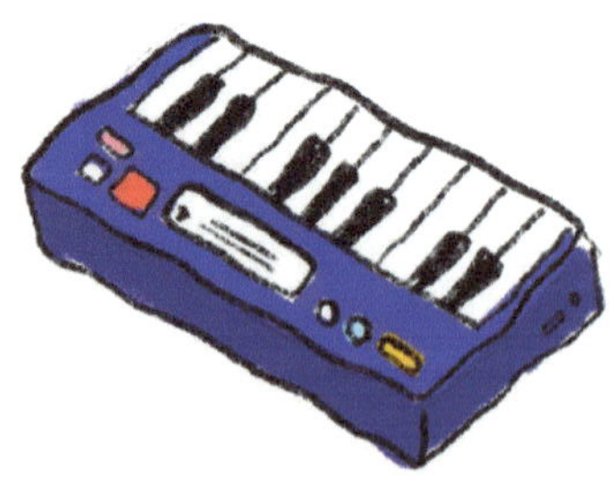

HEALTHY FOOD

Eating local & seasonal food significantly impacts balancing hormonal activity in the body. Create clean eating habits that exclude processed, packaged, and sugar-rich food options.

FREE PLAY

Free play means unstructured, child-led play time where the child decides the nature and course of play without any intervention from the adult except participation if the child intends it. Free play gives children enough time, space, and opportunity to work through their feelings and express them through play. This is a handy tool for younger children. For older children, this can be done through simple unstructured family time.

NURTURING ENVIRONMENT

Creating an environment that is Judgement free, inclusive, accepting, responsive & warm; fosters connection, secure attachment, & care; establishes good communication, support & guidance; allows for children to feel free and safe to express themselves and honestly communicate about what brings them joy and what unsettles them!

Here's an example of what incorporating the above in a day could look like!

Waking the children up to music in the morning and playing it through their morning routine. Scheduling an hour of outdoor playtime with lots of movement and elements of risky play in the evening. Scheduling half an hour of free play time just before bedtime and creating a warm bedtime routine to create a safe space for expressing themselves.

✦ **What lifestyle choices are already incorporated into your everyday routine?**

✦ **What are the ones you can incorporate right away?**

✦ **What support and resources would you need to incorporate the rest?**

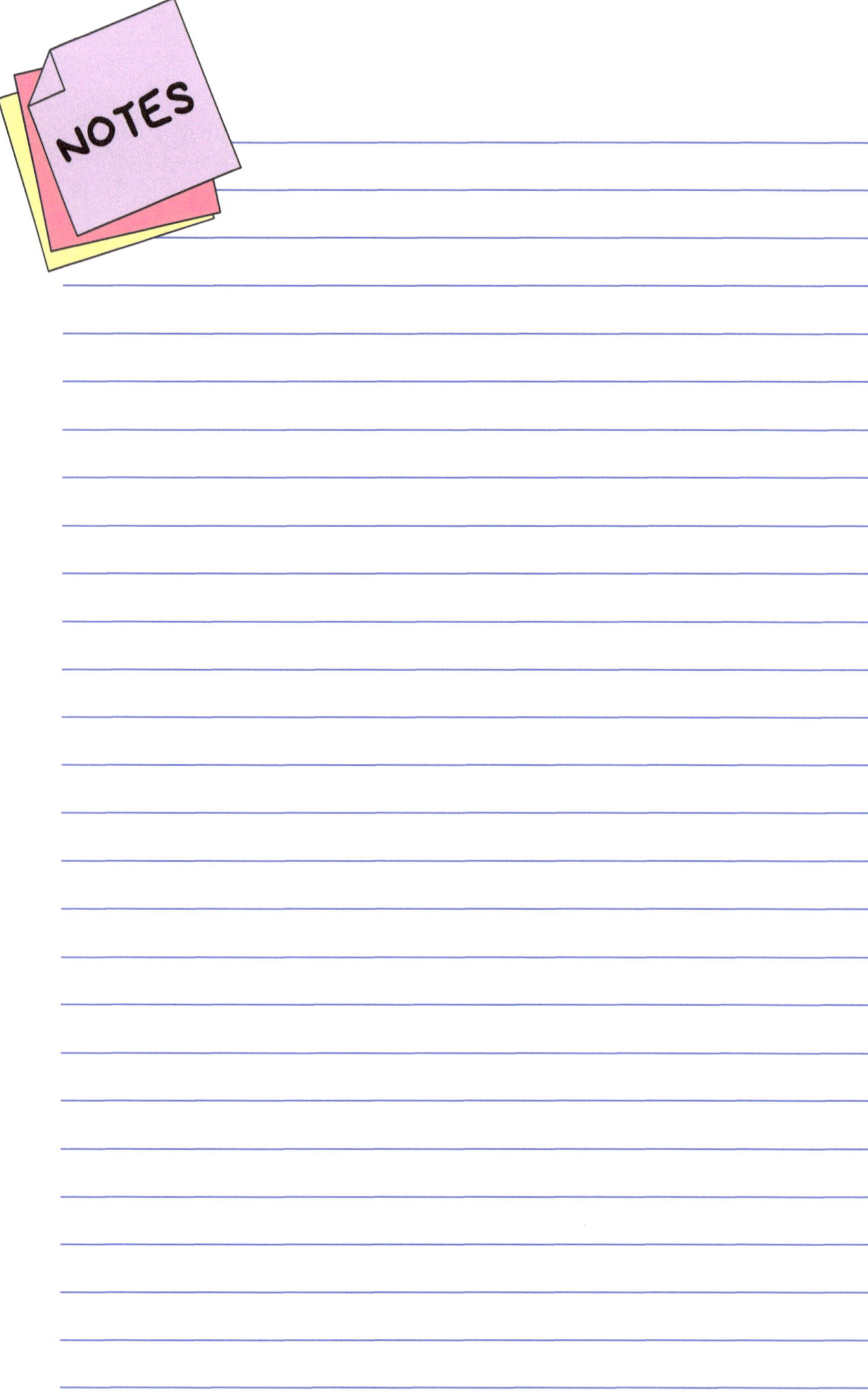
NOTES

HOW TO MODEL
EMOTIONAL INTELLIGENCE
TO CHILDREN

Building on and improving our emotional intelligence helps in nurturing emotional intelligence in children. Here are a few things that will not only help you improve or build your emotional intelligence but also a way to model emotional intelligence to your children.

LISTEN

If you want to understand the child's feelings, pay attention and listen to what the child is trying to tell you. Focus on both verbal and non-verbal communication. Dwell into different factors that might be contributing to that emotion.

EMPATHISE

Practice empathising with the child. It is critical to understand their point of view. Empathy is the quality that enables us to perceive another's experience and then communicate that perception back to the individual.

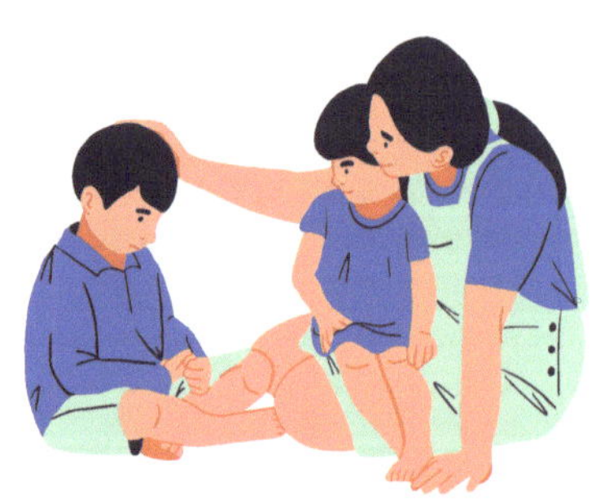

REFLECT

The ability to reason with emotions, i.e. how emotions influence thoughts and behaviours, helps us understand why the child feels a certain way and the factors that might contribute to these feelings.

Over the next few days, identify five disagreements between you and your children. Try the above routine with them each time. Journal your emotions, thoughts and responses for every step in the routine.

This could be an excellent way to build healthy communication channels with your other relationships, be it your partner, co-workers, friends, family or acquaintances!

SITUATION   **LISTEN**   **EMAPATHISE**   **REFLECT**

EMOTIONS

THOUGHTS

RESPONSES

EMOTIONS

THOUGHTS

RESPONSES

EMOTICNS

THOUGHTS

RESPONSES

EMOTIONS

THOUGHTS

RESPONSES

EMOTIONS

THOUGHTS

RESPONSES

NOTES

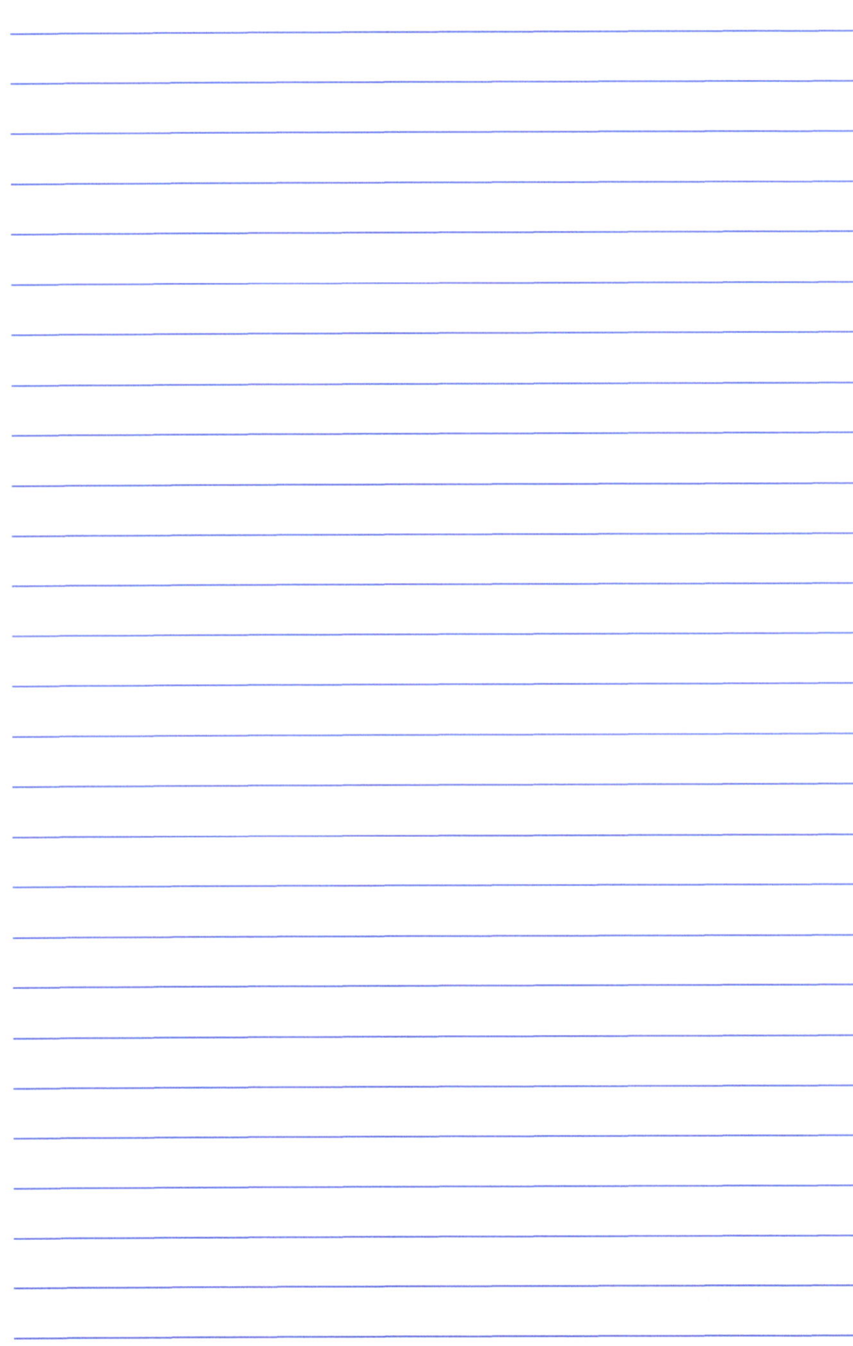

EMOTIONAL INTELLIGENCE

FREEDOM OF EXPRESSION

Children express both joy and discomfort uninhibitedly. While expression of joy generally seems acceptable, expressions of discomfort call for distraction, be it removing them from the environment or using toys when they are little to more substantial distractions when they are older and one day as adults, they'd be using distractions like binge eating or screen time to distract themselves from discomfort.

To allow for expression, children must be encouraged to let out their emotions and express the thoughts that cause them discomfort while discouraging aggressive or hostile actions or behaviour.

So, if an infant cries, a toddler has a tantrum, a child has an outburst, or a teenager has a mood swing, support them to ride these emotions without trying to distract them or problem-solving for them and express their thoughts. However, often such instances are accompanied by behaviours such as kicking, hitting, biting, slamming doors, throwing things and the like. While it is necessary to support children in working through their emotions, it is also essential that we lovingly inhibit associated behaviours and assert that while we acknowledge and accept their feelings, we may disagree with them.

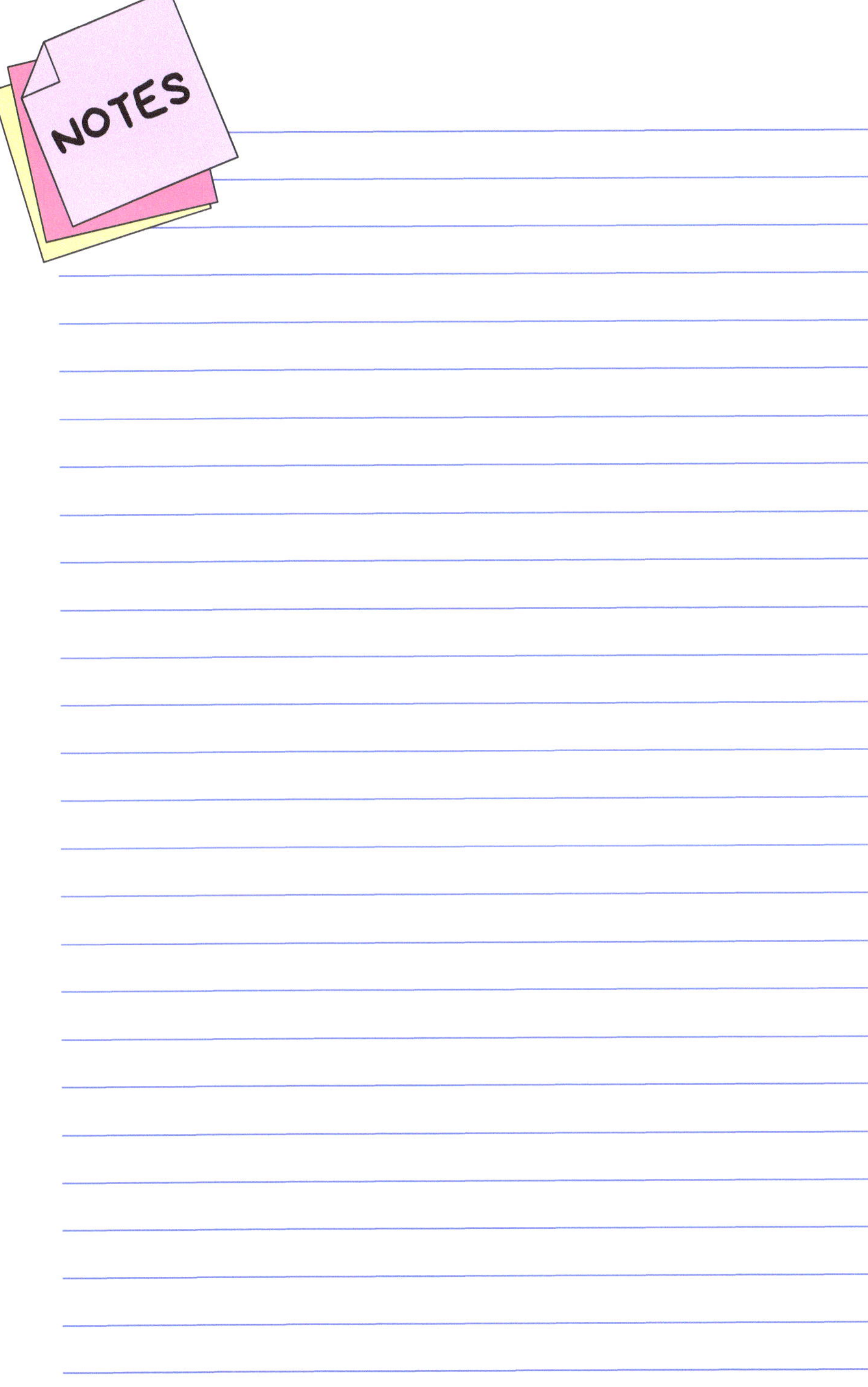
NOTES

SAFE ENVIRONMENT

For anyone, including children, to feel and express their emotions and thoughts, the most basic requirement is a safe space. Apart from having adequate measures for physical safety, the features of a safe space would include:

Accepting your child's emotions gives children the message that emotions are universal and manageable and help them release any discomfort they may feel. Disapproving their feelings will force them to repress them and may surface as behavioural issues, nightmares, loss of appetite, and the like.

Safe environments give children the opportunity to feel their emotions, express their thoughts, self-regulate their behaviours, reflect and enable problem-solving. Such children grow into enabled adults who are aware and empathetic.

RESPECT BOUNDARIES

As stated earlier, children are born with the uninhibited ability to express themselves. As a consequence, they set and communicate boundaries too. Often, these boundaries are crossed deliberately or by oversight. Circumstances that lead to deliberate crossing of these boundaries usually stem from the thought 'we know best', and events that lead to crossing the boundaries by oversight stem from the assumption 'this is what the child needs'. In either case, it's the lack of awareness. The reason for the lack of awareness is a conditioned mind that takes decisions based on rigid beliefs formed from past experiences.

When children express discomfort, they say 'No' and set boundaries. When we respect these boundaries, we acknowledge their emotions, accept their autonomy and validate their thoughts.:

Here are a few things we could do to ensure their boundaries are respected:

To respect their boundaries, we must first go through a journey of becoming aware and mindful! Listening and mindfulness help in understanding & respecting boundaries.

NOTES

LISTEN

With children, it is essential to be conscious and aware of verbal and non-verbal communication, changes in behaviour, variations in appetite, disturbed sleep, reduced attention span and the like:

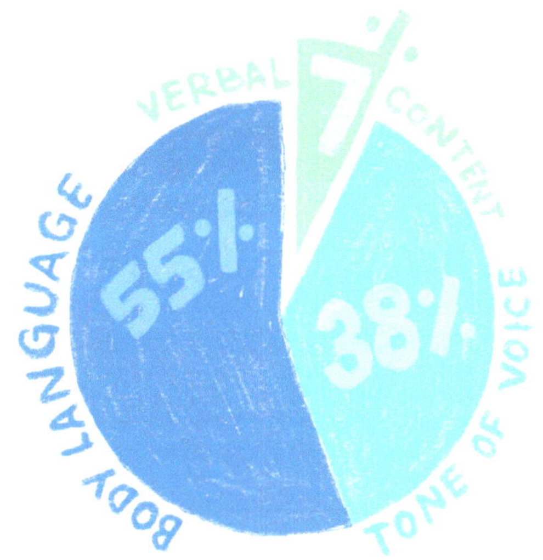

Specific indications of body language and nonverbal communication include:

- **Body Language in General: Posture; Facial expression; Gestures; Repetitive behaviours**

- **Body Language in Particular: The head; the eyes; the hands; the arms and legs; the skin**

- **Non-Verbal but Vocal Communication: The tone of voice; the rate of speech; the loudness of voice; the diction**

- **Other Non-Verbal Messages: Regarding time; regarding the other person's appearance, Appetite, Sleep Patterns**

Listening with proper understanding is inherent in all of us and the most essential skill in helping. Here are a few guidelines that will help us be present and help children feel they are being listened to:

 **Be present.** Here it's not only about physical presence but also being mentally present without any distractions or preconceived notions that drive us towards judgements. This can be done by doing away with, or at least diminishing, internal distractions, such as your ideas, interests, concerns, and all that make up your frame of reference.

 Physically attend to the other person. Sit to look at or hold your child comfortably at an eye-to-eye level.

 Ensure the environment is free from external distractions, such as noises, objects and interruptions.

 Focus on the child's feelings as they share their story and emotional problems or in younger children, while they cry.

 Show acceptance of those feelings by permitting the child to feel their feelings, whether good or bad, right or wrong, directed at others, themselves, or even us.

 Limit your questions to clarifying a point ('Is this what you are trying to say?'). Never ask questions out of curiosity or from feeling uncomfortable with the child's silence, especially with older children.

 Be comfortable with silence. Silences are capable of bringing forth new insights. Allow such silences without interrupting the reflection because of your uneasiness.

Once kids (and adults) feel their emotions are acknowledged, accepted, and listened to, the feelings lose their charge and begin to dissipate. This leaves an opening for problem-solving. Help them only if they ask you to. This gives them the message that you have confidence in their abilities.

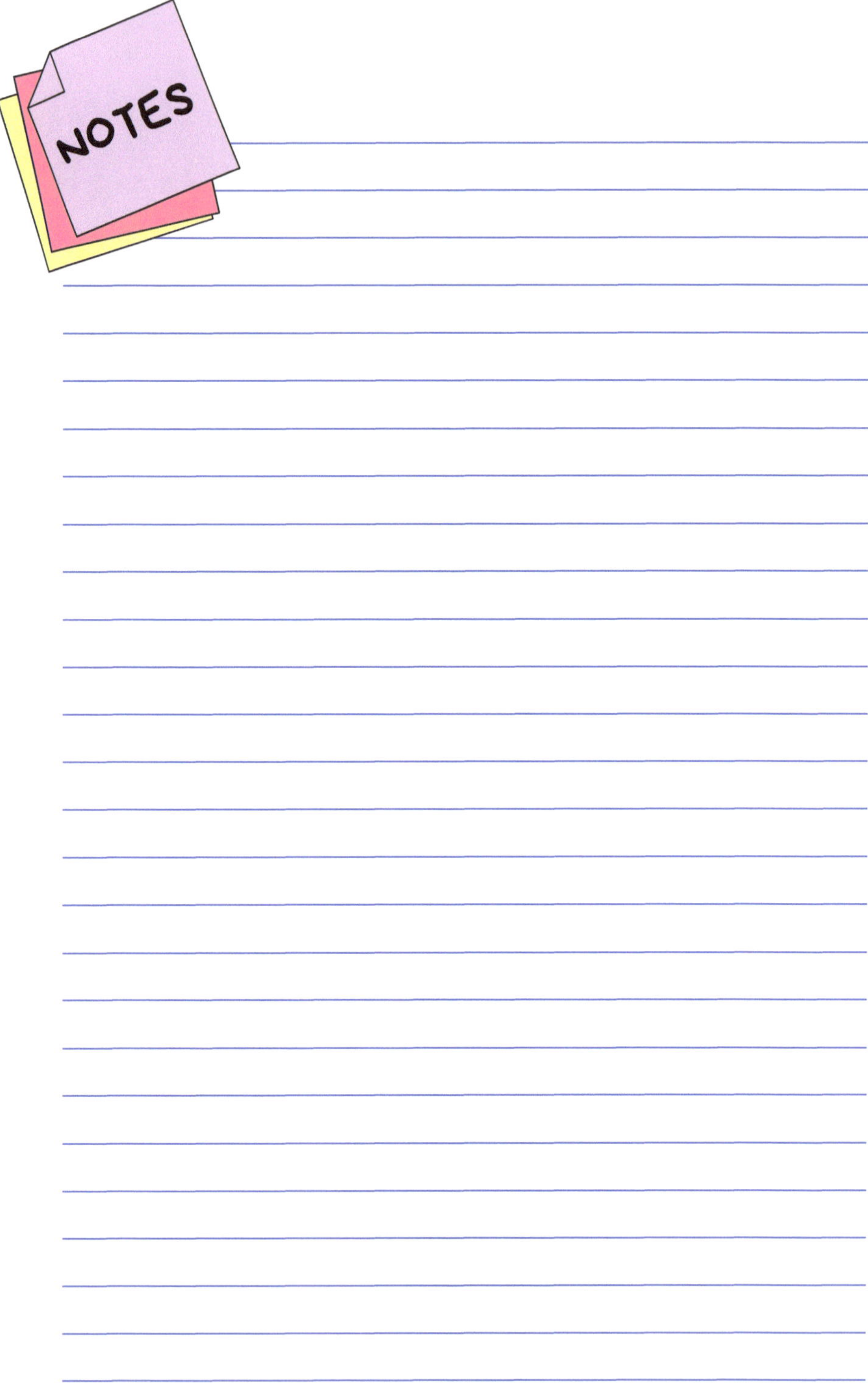
NOTES

PLAY

Play is another essential tool for developing emotional intelligence in children, especially when you notice a negative pattern developing. It could indicate that your child has unprocessed feelings they don't know how to handle. Here play would mean free play!

Free play means unstructured, child-led play time where the child decides the nature and course of play without any intervention from the adult except participation if the child intends it.

Free play gives children enough time, space and opportunity to work through their feelings and express them through play. This is a handy tool for younger children. For older children, this can be done through simple unstructured family time.

For instance, your four-year-old always wants Mommy. Help him understand why he needs to cling to Mommy by providing adequate time for free play. When children are given the security, space and freedom to express themselves, they do it through play.

Your four-year-old may pick up a doll, pretend for the doll to be him and him to be the Mommy and through the doll, express why he feels the need to be around Mommy all the time, or this may even happen through a direct conversation.

Here are a few ways to incorporate and use free play or unstructured time.

★ Free play time is the time that does not include screen time, structured playtime, lessons time or any other scheduled time that involves instructions or structure.

★ Set aside some time every day or every week; the critical point is at equal frequencies for free play or unstructured time.

★ Check with the child about what the child would like to do during that time. Decide this in advance so you can make all the arrangements to ensure the time is used to its full potential.

★ Listen and observe what the child expresses through play; it could simply be joy or sometimes pain, discomfort, sadness, anger and the like. Use the guidelines under Listen to help you with this.

★ Respond with empathy by reflecting and rephrasing what they were expressing through play. This would help them feel safe and comfortable.

Over the next few days, consciously list down five situations when your child hasn't fully expressed themselves; for each situation, what could be the reasons for their inhibitions? which of the above tools would help your child express better based on the reasons. Take the time to think through and detail how the tools could be implemented to help your child better.

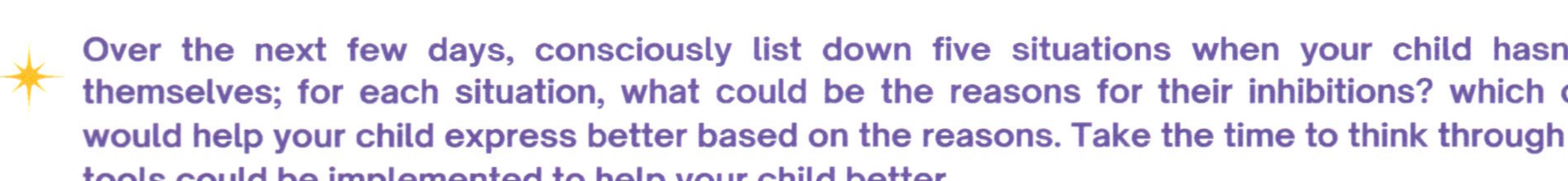

Situation	Reasons for Inhibitions	What tools could be used and how

NOTES

HOW DO WE FRAME A
RESPONSE
WHILE DEALING WITH A
CHILD'S EMOTIONS

Dealing with emotionally charged children can be challenging. Having your responses handy to support them while dealing with their emotions is always good. The key is to name the emotion, affirm to them that having these emotions are human while inhibiting any aggressive or untoward behaviour, reassure them that you are going to be right there with them, listening to whatever they have to say and encourage them to find a solution to their predicament!

1. BREATHE

A simple breathing technique to breathe in through the nose and breathe out through the mouth can help self-regulate.

2. IDENTIFYING FEELINGS

Help children understand and name different feelings to identify their feelings. For the older ones, we can use the feelings wheel created by Dr Gloria Willcox.

3. SETTING BOUNDARIES

Help them by boundaries by inhibiting aggressive or untoward behaviour.

4. ENCOURAGE PROBLEM SOLVING

Problem-solving builds a child's self-confidence and helps them become more resilient.

5. REFLECT

Help children consider how their emotions influence their decisions and behaviours through reflective questions. This helps them better understand emotions' role in thinking and behaving.

Here are a few examples of using the above to frame your responses.

Try these techniques and see how much closer you feel with your child - your child's emotional intelligence can be developed and nurtured through empathy, listening, modelling play and creating a safe environment.

Identify 5 difficult situations that you faced with your child and draft a response that you would like to use using the above prompts

SITUATION	RESPONSES

BIBLIOGRAPHY

https://www.verywellmind.com/what-is-emotional-intelligence-2795423

https://www.medicalnewstoday.com/articles/low-emotional-lintelligence#signs-of-low-ei

Parivarthan's Listening Skills Technique
Level - 1

NOTES

RESOURCES

FEELING

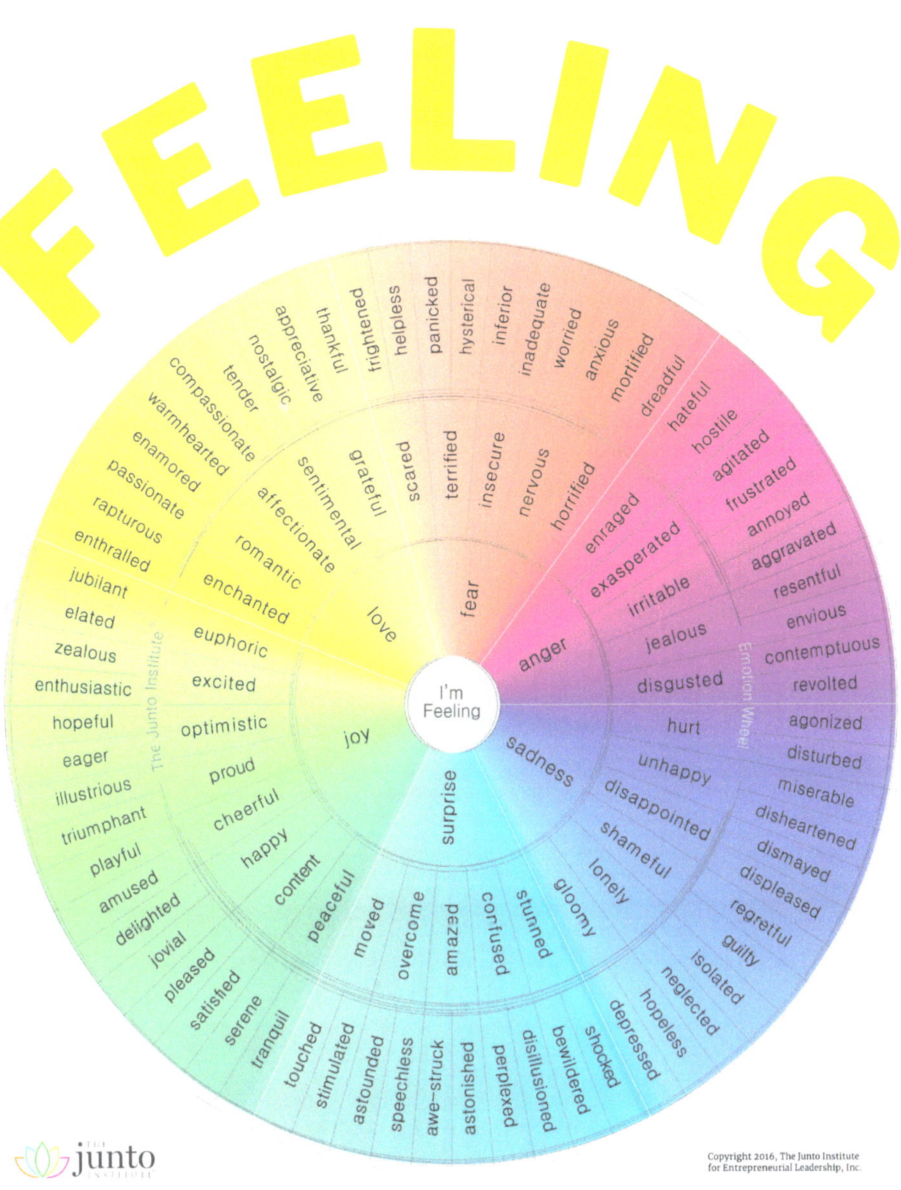

WHEEL

SAFE ENVIRONMENT

RESPECT BOUNDARIES

Bhavana Nagendra is a Chartered Accountant with over 10 years of experience. In retrospect what she really did like about her job was the opportunity to coach and mentor those on her team to understand their calling, set goals and create an action plan to achieve their goals!

In 2019, when she had her daughter, AJ, she knew she wanted to be a part of AJ's every growing moment. She took a break from her career and spent the days with AJ. Being with AJ had her understand her values, question her belief systems, and restructure her life based on what mattered the most – living and being in the moment. As AJ was growing, it occurred to her that the schooling system as is wouldn't do justice to help AJ continue being a curious little explorer and learn as naturally as she was. One of the options she came across was home-schooling and it was at this time that the funder of an NGO and an alternative education school, working with underprivileged children decided to launch a program for parents to understand a child's learning journey. Initially she had hoped to participate in the program but after her initial discussion with the founder, she was given the opportunity to co-create and co-facilitate the program. The irony of the program was that it had nothing to do with children but worked on the belief systems of the parents – something she had learnt in her journey as a parent.

The success of the program inspired her to get her Professional Coach Certification (PCC) from the ICF (International Coaching Federation). Her work is based on positive psychology, spiritual growth, self-reflection, understanding values, questioning belief systems, unlearning, unconditioning, acceptance and mindfulness. She is currently a visiting faculty at one of the KFI group schools and continues home-schooling AJ. She is a minimalist and has implemented a sustainable lifestyle in her urban home.

She is currently pursuing her Master's in Psychology and Master Coach Certification to continue creating positive powerful impact in the lives that she crosses paths with!

In continuation of her quest to find a learning space that promotes freedom, acceptance and the joy of learning she has now created Svadhyaya's Learning Space.

With over 500 hours of coaching experience, I consider it my privilege and I am grateful to be able to partner with, coach and empower people who wish to grow personally and professionally as a Life Empowerment Coach! In all this time I have also learnt, grown and transformed with each one of the individuals I have coached - a true partnership indeed.

To know more about Coaching Sessions and Programs at the Learning Space reach out to us at:

@bhavna.nagendra   www.theartofsvadhyaya.com   @theartofsvadhyaya

www.ingramcontent.com/pod-product-compliance
Lightning Source LLC
Chambersburg PA
CBHW040945110726
48006CB00007B/1261